# Animals, Animals, Animals

*Written and illustrated by Martha Rohrer*

Copyright 2004
**Rod and Staff Publishers, Inc.**
P.O. Box 3, Highway 172
Crockett, Kentucky 41413
**Telephone (606) 522-4348**

Printed in U.S.A.

ISBN 978-07399-2348-1
Catalog no. 2950

The cow gives milk for us to drink;

The sheep eats grass so green.

The goat may also give us milk;

The kitten licks it clean.

The puppy likes to play and bark.

We like to ride the horse.

The donkey too may give us rides.

The pig likes mud, of course.

Some animals are not so tame;
They hide when we come near.

The chipmunk runs into his hole.

There stands a graceful deer.

The fox comes slyly from her den.

The squirrel plays in the tree.

The masked raccoon goes to the stream.

The skunk is striped, you see.

The porcupine has prickly quills.

The beaver swims and gnaws.

The woodchuck watches near his hole.

The rabbit licks his paws.

The bear eats berries, ants, and fish.

The bobcat hunts at night,

While far away the zebra roams.

A lion causes fright.

The camel plods across the sand.

An elephant is seen.

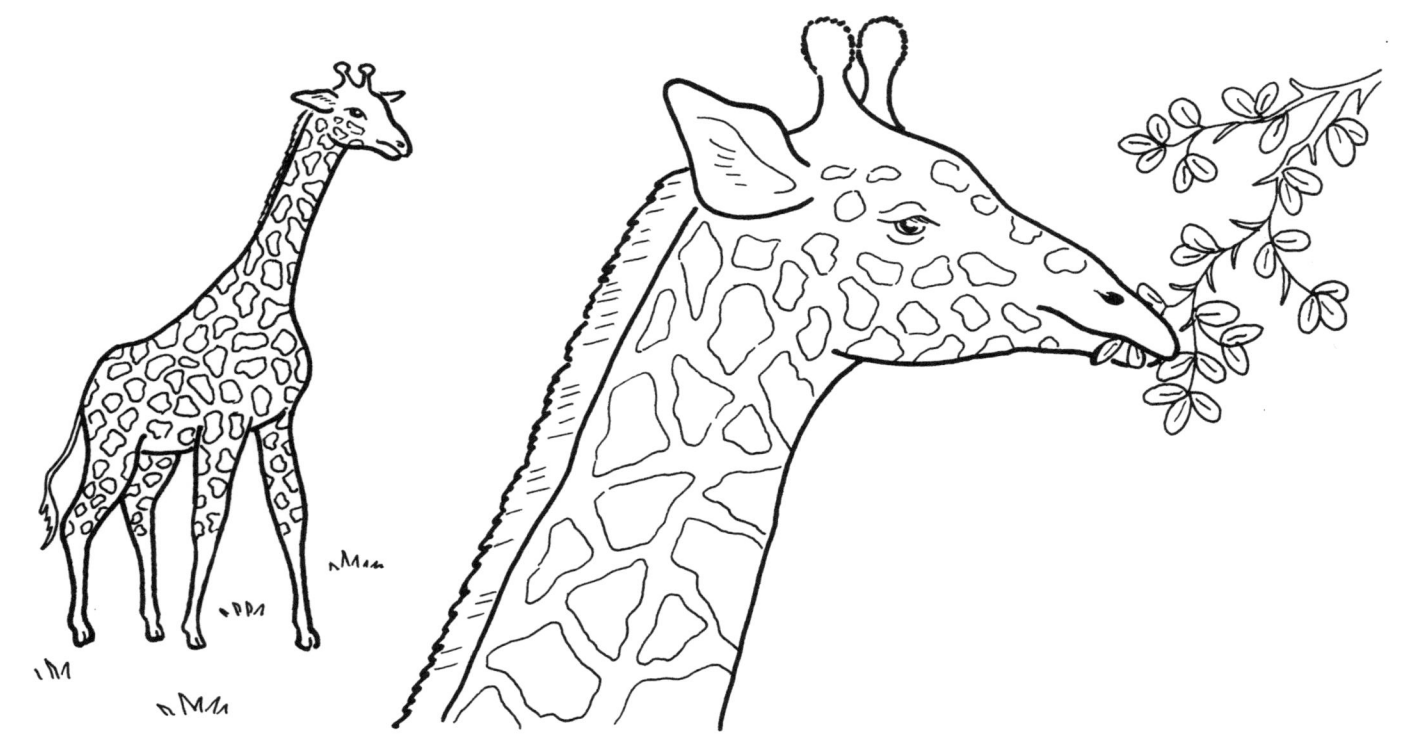

A tall giraffe eats leaves so high.

The tiger's ears are keen.

The kangaroo takes great big jumps.

The monkeys climb the trees,

While dolphins swim in oceans warm,

And seals in icy seas.

jack rabbit

sloth

armadillo

koala

moose

mountain sheep

God made so many animals
That live in different ways;
They live in different places too,
But all can bring Him praise.

# I Used To Be Afraid Of... Spiders

Whose strange-looking face is this? Sharp fangs, beady little eyes—it's a spider! A creepy spider could be anywhere. It could be in the garden. It could be in your house!

Many spiders are small. But this hairy, scary spider is bigger than your fist! It is a tarantula. Like all spiders, it has eight legs.

If a spider crawled up your arm right now, would you yell and jump with fright? Spiders scare many people. But most spiders are not harmful. They even help people.

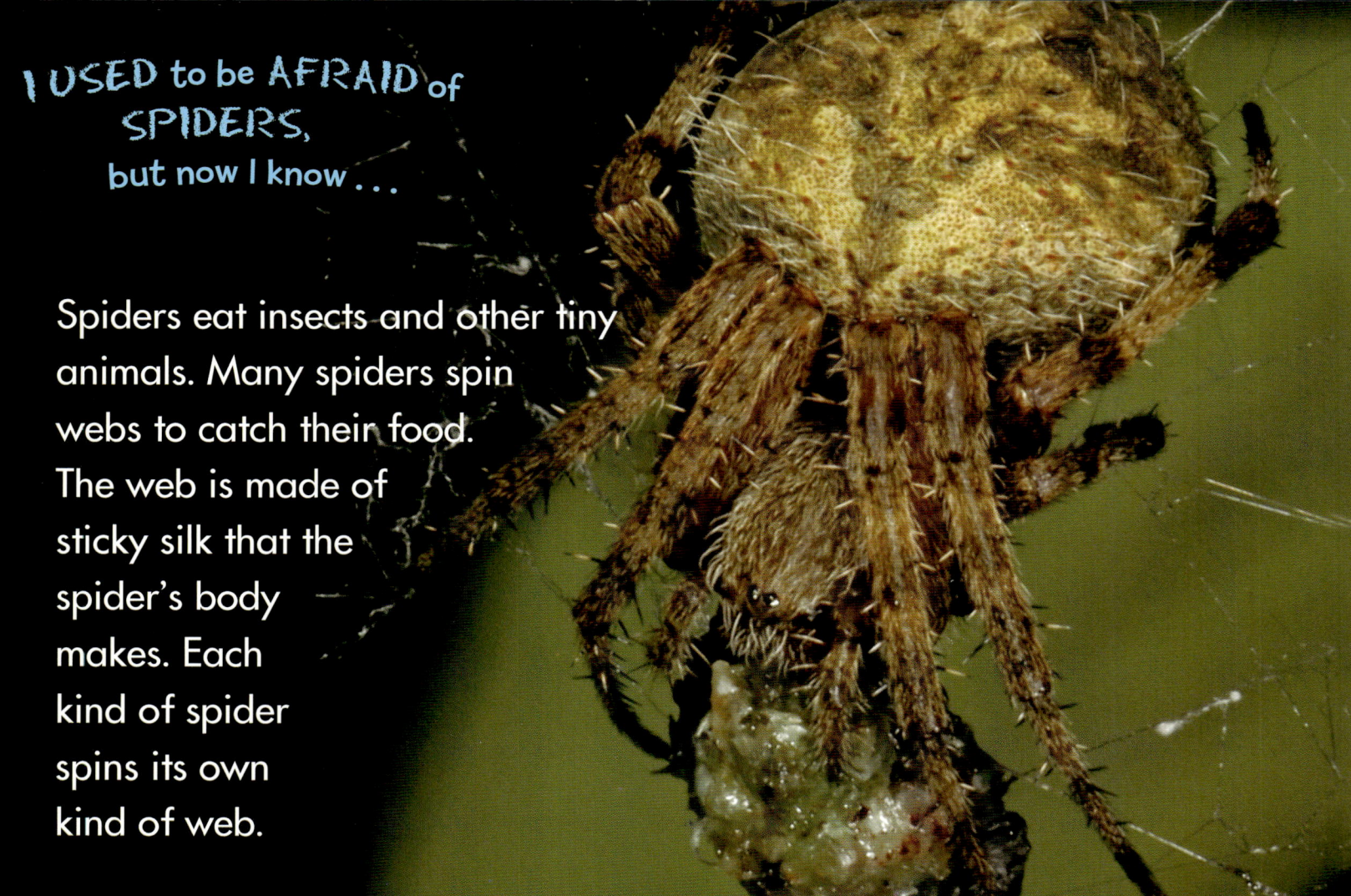

I USED to be AFRAID of SPIDERS, but now I know...

Spiders eat insects and other tiny animals. Many spiders spin webs to catch their food. The web is made of sticky silk that the spider's body makes. Each kind of spider spins its own kind of web.

Some webs look like wheels. Some look like funnels. If an insect enters the web, it is caught. The spider rushes over and bites the insect. Then the spider binds its prey in strands of silk.

I USED to be AFRAID of SPIDERS, but now I know . . .

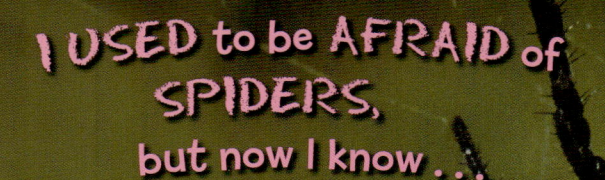

This yellow and black garden spider is a web weaver. She also uses her silk to protect her eggs. The spider lays her eggs in fall.

She weaves a pear-shaped sac around them. Tiny spiderlings hatch from the eggs. They stay in the silken nest until spring. When they have grown a bit, the spiderlings crawl out.

I USED to be AFRAID of SPIDERS, but now I know...

The jumping spider wraps her eggs in silk, too. She stays nearby to guard the eggs until they hatch. She looks fierce, doesn't she?

The wolf spider carries her eggs wherever she goes. And when the spiderlings hatch, they ride around on her back! They jump off when they are big enough to live on their own.

**I USED to be AFRAID of SPIDERS, but now I know . . .**

Jumping spiders don't weave webs. But like all spiders, they are hunters. They pounce on their prey, like tiny tigers.

The spider spins a single thread of silk as it jumps. The silk thread will catch the spider if it falls. Spider silk is super strong.

I USED to be AFRAID of SPIDERS, but now I know...

Spiders are helpful to people. But they are bad news for insects. Spiders eat insects that harm farm crops and garden plants.

Without spiders, there would be more insect pests. Spiders even eat other spiders, too!

I USED to be AFRAID of SPIDERS,
but now I know...

Spiders are also food for other
animals, such as birds, wasps, snakes,
and frogs. But a hungry bird may pass right
by and never see this spider.

Some spiders can hide in plain sight. Their colors match the plants where they hang out. This allows them to sneak up on insects they want to catch.

**I USED to be AFRAID of SPIDERS, but now I know...**

All spiders can bite. But they will not bite unless bothered. Only a few spiders, like this black widow, have bites that are harmful to people. Spiders are fun to watch. Let them weave their webs in peace, and you won't need to be afraid.